# Contents

# Leeds Castle

## Maidstone · Kent

THE
West Prospect of Leeds Castle

Published on behalf of the Foundation
by Philip Wilson Publishers Limited,
Russell Chambers, Covent Garden,
London WC2E 8AA

ISBN 0 85667 208 4

Printed in England by
Jolly and Barber Limited, Rugby

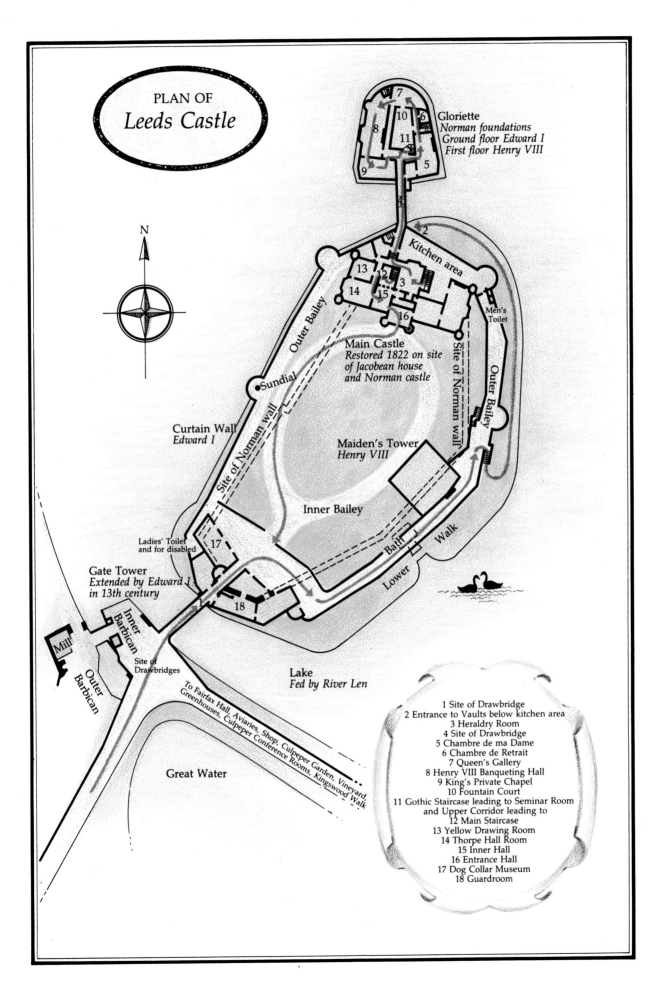

PLAN OF
**Leeds Castle**

N

Gloriette
*Norman foundations*
*Ground floor Edward I*
*First floor Henry VIII*

7
10  6
8
11
9  5
4
2
Kitchen area
13  12
14  15  3
16
Men's Toilet

Outer Bailey

Sundial

Main Castle
*Restored 1822 on site*
*of Jacobean house*
*and Norman castle*

Curtain Wall
*Edward I*

Maiden's Tower
*Henry VIII*

Site of Norman wall

Outer Bailey

Site of Norman wall

Inner Bailey

Ladies' Toilet
and for disabled

17

Bath  Walk

Lower  Walk

Gate Tower
*Extended by Edward I*
*in 13th century*

18

Inner Barbican

Mill

Site of
Drawbridges

Outer Barbican

Lake
*Fed by River Len*

To Fairfax Hall, Aviaries, Shop, Culpeper Garden, Vineyard,
Greenhouses, Culpeper Conference Rooms, Kingswood Walk

Great Water

1 Site of Drawbridge
2 Entrance to Vaults below kitchen area
3 Heraldry Room
4 Site of Drawbridge
5 Chambre de ma Dame
6 Chambre de Retrait
7 Queen's Gallery
8 Henry VIII Banqueting Hall
9 King's Private Chapel
10 Fountain Court
11 Gothic Staircase leading to Seminar Room
and Upper Corridor leading to
12 Main Staircase
13 Yellow Drawing Room
14 Thorpe Hall Room
15 Inner Hall
16 Entrance Hall
17 Dog Collar Museum
18 Guardroom

# Chronology of Owners

## Holders of the Manor of Leeds

| | |
|---|---|
| Ethelbert IV (under King of Kent) | |
| Earl Godwin | 856-860 |
| Earl Lewin | 1052-1053 |
| William I (The Conqueror) | 1053-1066 |
| Odo, Earl of Kent, Bishop of Bayeau | 1066 |
| William II (Rufus) | 1066-1090 |
| Hamon de Crèvecoeur | |
| Etard de Crèvecoeur | between 1090-1119 |

*1066 October 14 Battle of Hastings*

## Holders of Leeds Castle and the Manor of Leeds

*1086 Domesday Survey*

| | |
|---|---|
| Robert de Crèvecoeur | |
| Daniel de Crèvecoeur | |
| Robert de Crèvecoeur | |
| Hamon de Crèvecoeur | |
| Hamon de Crèvecoeur | d.1242 |
| Robert de Crèvecoeur | 1242-1268 |
| Sir Roger de Leyburn | 1268-1271 |
| Lord William de Leyburn | 1271-1278 |
| Eleanor of Castile | 1278-1290 |
| Edward I | 1290-1297 |
| Lady Isabel de Vescy | 1297-1299 |
| Margaret of France | 1299-1317 |
| Lord Bartholomew de Badlesmere | 1317-1321 |
| Edward II | 1321-1327 |
| Isabella of France | 1327-1358 |
| Edward III | 1358-1377 |
| Richard II | 1377-1382 |
| Anne of Bohemia | 1382-1394 |
| Lady Joan de Mohun | 1394-1399 |
| Henry IV | 1399 |
| Sir John Norbury | 1399-1403 |
| Joan of Navarre | 1403-1412 |
| Thomas Arundel, | |
|    Archbishop of Canterbury | 1412-1414 |
| Joan Countess of Hereford | 1414-1419 |
| Henry V | 1419-1422 |
| Catherine de Valois | 1422-1437 |
| Sir John Steward | 1437-1449 |
| Henry VI | 1449-1461 |
| Edward IV | 1461-1483 |
| Edward V | 1483 |
| Richard III | 1483-1485 |
| Henry VII | 1485-1509 |
| Henry VIII | 1509-1547 |
| Edward VI | 1547-1552 |

*c.1120 Commencement of first stone castle on site*

*1139 The Empress Matilda invades England. First siege of castle.*

*1265 Battle of Evesham*

*1278 Leeds Castle conveyed to the Crown*

*1321 Second siege of castle*

*1358-1377 Creation of the 'beautiful palace in Kent'*

*1395 Froissart visits Richard II at the castle*

*1412 Trial of Sir John Oldcastle in absentia*

*1444 Trial of Eleanor Cobham, Duchess of Gloucester*

*1485 Battle of Bosworth*

*1517-1522 Restoration of the fabric*

*1520 Field of the Cloth of Gold*

*1552 Castle alienated by the Crown*

## Private Owners of Leeds Castle

| | | |
|---|---|---|
| Sir Anthony St Leger | 1552-1559 | *1607 First permanent settlement in Virginia* |
| Sir Warham St Leger | 1559-1597 | |
| Anthony St Leger, Esq. | 1597-1602 | |
| Sir Warham St Leger | 1602-1618 | *1618 Rebuilding of main residence* |
| Sir Richard Smith | 1618-1628 | |
| Sir John Smith | 1628-1632 | |
| Lady Elizabeth Thornhill and Mrs Mary Barrow | 1632 | *1641 Outbreak of Civil War* |
| Sir Thomas Culpeper | 1632 | *1660 Restoration of the Monarchy* |
| Sir Cheney Culpeper | 1632-1663 | |
| Thomas 2nd Lord Culpeper | 1663-1689 | *1776 American Declaration of Independence* |
| Margaret Lady Culpeper | 1689-1710 | |
| Catherine Lady Fairfax | 1710-1719 | |
| Thomas 6th Lord Fairfax | 1719-1747 | *1822-1825 Massive rebuilding and restoration programme* |
| Robert Fairfax, afterwards 7th Lord | 1747-1793 | |
| Revd Dr Denny (Martin) Fairfax | 1793-1800 | |
| General Philip Martin R.A. | 1800-1821 | *1914 Officers of B.E.F. entertained on their march to Folkestone* |
| Fiennes Wykeham-Martin Esq. | 1821-1840 | |
| Charles Wykeham-Martin Esq. M.P. | 1840-1870 | |
| Philip Wykeham-Martin Esq. M.P. | 1870-1878 | |
| Mrs Elizabeth Wykeham-Martin | 1878-1893 | *1927-1929 Initial restoration of the fabric by Lady Baillie* |
| Cornwallis Philip Wykeham-Martin Esq. | 1893-1924 | |
| Fairfax Wykeham-Martin Esq. | 1924-1926 | *Exactly when the Manor of Leeds came into the gift of the Saxon royal line cannot at present be determined* |
| Hon. Olive Lady Baillie | 1926-1974 | |

## Owner in Perpetuity

Leeds Castle Foundation from 1974

*The line of the de Crèvecoeur family is taken from a fragment found in the Filmer mss.*

The Arms of Edward I
and Queen Eleanor of Castile

The Arms of the Hon. Lady Baillie

In this aerial view of Leeds Castle set in its wooded landscape, the layout of the buildings can be clearly seen – a panorama of architecture from the twelfth to the twentieth centuries. On the extreme left of the complex is the thirteenth-century Gloriette, its walls rising sheer from the water of the lake and connected to the main island by stone passages. The main island itself is bounded on the left by a revetment wall with two drum bastions, again rising high out of the water, dating from *c*1280. At the northern end of the island is the main part of the castle, rebuilt in the nineteenth century to replace a Jacobean building, which in turn had replaced medieval buildings on the same site. The Maiden's Tower, the square building on the right, was constructed in the late Tudor period, while the main group of buildings in the foreground, through which the main entrance road passes, dates from the same period as the Gloriette. The Gate Tower is a late Norman structure, improved upon by Edward I and surviving in that style today, while in the small courtyard to which it leads, the buildings originally used as coach houses and stables in Edward's time now house the Dog Collar Museum. The path running along the narrow causeway which separates the surrounding lake from the Great Water leads to the gardens, aviaries and Fairfax Hall, just visible beyond the trees.

'Leeds, beheld among the waters on an autumnal evening when the bracken is golden and there is a faint blue mist among the trees - the loveliest castle, as thus beheld, in the whole world.'

# Foreword
## by Sir Arthur Bryant CH

RAISED ON AN ISLAND on the site of a Kentish thane's stronghold, Leeds
Castle, oldest and most romantic of England's 'stately homes', was first
built in stone by a Norman baron in the reign of William the Conqueror's
son, Henry I, nearly nine hundred years ago. A century and a half later,
on the accession of Edward I – the King whose adage that what concerns
all should be approved by all, makes him, more than any other of our
sovereigns, the real founder of our Parliament – this formidable baronial
fortress, as it then was, came into the possession of the Crown. For the
next three centuries a royal palace and the 'lady's castle' of six of England's
medieval queens, it later passed, through royal grant and subsequent
purchases, into the hands of three famous English families – the St. Legers,
the Culpepers and the Fairfaxes – until, in our own century, it was bought
from its then owners, the Wykeham-Martins, by Lady Baillie – daughter,
by his American Whitney wife, of my old friend the late Almeric Paget,
Lord Queenborough, whose grandfather commanded the British cavalry at
Waterloo. It was Olive Baillie's lifelong love for, and devoted restoration
of, this ancient and beautiful castle with its lovely park and gardens,
together with her vision and generosity which, after a lapse of four
centuries, has brought about its re-dedication to the service of the nation.

It is strange how often the history of this romantic castle has impinged
on the wider history of both England and America. The earliest of the
Queens whose loved home it was, was the Spanish princess Eleanor of
Castile, who saved the life of her crusading husband after he was struck
down by an assassin's poisoned dagger at Acre. Edward's love for this
noble, stately woman, with her long, dark, Spanish tresses and calm
Gothic features, proved the guiding star of his life, the happiest part of
which was spent with her at Leeds Castle. 'My harp is turned to
mourning,' he wrote after she died, 'in life I loved her dearly, nor can I

11

cease to love her in death.' At every place where her bier rested on its journey to Westminster, he raised a cross in her memory, the name of the last of which, the *chère reine* (or Charing) cross, has survived in that of the London thoroughfare where Dr. Johnson maintained that the full tide of human existence was best to be encountered.

Another royal romance associated with Leeds Castle was that of Queen Catherine de Valois – widow of Henry V and the 'French Kate' of Shakespeare's play – who, while living there, fell in love with and secretly married her Clerk of the Wardrobe, an obscure but handsome young Welsh squire named Owen Tudor. The offspring of this concealed and scandalous match, as it seemed to contemporaries, was the father of Henry Tudor, who, after his victory at Bosworth Field, became, as Henry VII, the founder of the greatest of all England's historic dynasties. It was to Leeds Castle, too, that the first Tudor's still more famous son, Henry VIII, brought Ann Boleyn, whose 'great key' was long preserved there. Henry later enriched Leeds with its noble banqueting hall.

Froissart in his *Chronicles* recorded his attendance on King Richard II in his 'beautiful palace in Kent called Leeds Castle', which that tragic king afterwards gave to his child bride, Anne of Bohemia. Edward VIII, when Prince of Wales, was a guest here in the days of its last chatelaine, Lady Baillie; and, during the second world war, Field Marshal Montgomery and Sir Bertram Ramsay, the Admiral who commanded the Allied naval operations on D Day, were among those who came on their wartime business to this great towered haunt of ancient peace and 'battles long ago', still dreaming in its encircling lake.

Perhaps the most extraordinary of all the castle's historic associations is that with the United States. One of its owners, Sir Warham St. Leger, was closely associated with Sir Walter Raleigh, the man whose lifelong dream – one for which he died on the scaffold – had been to found a new English nation on the far side of the Atlantic. During his starveling and perilous years of exile, Charles II rewarded one of his followers, Lord Culpeper, for his fidelity by a grant of more than five million acres of virgin American soil, so making him the 'Lord Proprietor' of what was to become the heartland of colonial North America. He and his immediate heirs were the greatest landowners known to American history. The last of them, the 6th Lord Fairfax – a relative of the victor of Marston Moor and Naseby – emigrated to America during the reign of George II, and was the friend and first employer of the young George Washington, who helped to survey part of his vast under-developed estates on the wild western Virginian frontier. After he had become the leader of an independent American nation, Washington praised 'the good old lord' who, living to the age of 89, carried on in the New World the traditions of generosity, liberality and good neighbourliness which he had learnt in youth at Leeds Castle.

Now the wheel of history has come full circle, and Lady Baillie, with the help of the inheritance from her American Whitney mother, has provided under her will that this wonderful Norman castle, whose former owner left it to follow his fortunes in the New World, is to be preserved in perpetuity for the public benefit as a centre of the arts, of charitable work and, in particular, for medical research in peaceful surroundings by the great physicians and scientists of all nations. No lovelier spot on earth could be found for such a purpose.

'Wonderful in manifold glories,' wrote the historian of castles, Lord Conway, 'are the great castle visions of Europe; Windsor from the Thames, Warwick or Ludlow from their riversides, Conway or Carnarvon from the sea, Amboise from the Loire, Aigues Mortes from the lagoons, Carcassonne, Coucy, Falaise and Chateau Gaillard – beautiful as they are and crowned with praise, are not comparable in beauty with Leeds, beheld among the waters on an autumnal evening when the bracken is golden and there is a faint blue mist among the trees – the loveliest castle, as thus beheld, in the whole world.'

# History of Leeds Castle

LEDIAN, OR LEED, was Chief Minister of Ethelbert IV, King of Kent, and a man with an eye to the safety of his family in troubled times. One day he noticed that, in a natural hollow on his land, the River Len had formed a large lake surrounding two islands. On these he built his wooden castle in 857, protecting it by placing a drawbridge over the water. Thus Leeds Castle was born over 1100 years ago.

Bishop Asser wrote of King Ethelbert, a brother of Alfred the Great: 'He governed with love and honour'. This was high praise in a rough age, and it casts a warm and ennobling radiance over those distant Saxon rulers, King Ethelbert and Leed, his Chief Minister. So the castle was first built by a good man and it has remained to this day, as Lady Baillie used to say, 'a happy castle'.

After the Conquest, the victorious Norman commanders at once realised the military value of the site of the Saxon fort. The Norman barons were surrounded and vastly outnumbered by the hostile English, so they held down the conquered country by building strong castles. William the Conqueror created his half-brother, Bishop Odo of Bayeux, Earl of Kent and gave him the manor of Leeds. In 1090, however, Odo rebelled and was exiled. The King then gave Leeds to his cousin, Hamon de Crèvecoeur, a Norman baron who had fought on the right flank of William the Conqueror's army at the Battle of Hastings.

In 1119 Robert de Crèvecoeur started building the stone castle, and also Leeds Priory, to house twenty Canons of the Order of St. Augustine. Some thirty de Crèvecoeurs were buried in the Priory, where there was a chantry for their souls - one of the earliest recorded. The Priory became one of the richest in Kent and gave hospitality to pilgrims on their way to the shrine of St. Thomas Becket at Canterbury. The Priory, alas, was destroyed under Henry VIII, but the site, which is near Leeds village, has recently been excavated by the Kent Archaeological Society.

For more than two hundred years after the Conquest the de Crèvecoeurs ruled over Leeds Castle and the Priory. They had gained the estate by fighting and they never really stopped fighting.

Following Henry I's death, King Stephen and his cousin Matilda contested the crown, and in 1139 Matilda invaded England with the help of her brother Robert, Earl of Gloucester. Robert held Leeds Castle for her for a time, but Kent was loyal to King Stephen and the King soon had the castle under his control.

Later, in the reign of King John, Hamo de Crèvecoeur, great-grandson of the Robert de Crèvecoeur who had originally built the castle, joined the rebellious barons, though he subsequently redeemed himself by paying a fine to Henry III. He married Matilda, the great heiress of William d'Averenche, and enormously increased his feudal power and wealth. However, his son Robert fought against the King at the Battle of Lewes and, when Henry III won the decisive Battle of Evesham in 1265, the family fortunes went into decline. Robert de Crèvecoeur was obliged to yield Leeds Castle to Sir Roger de Leyburn, a devoted friend and supporter of Henry III, and it was his son William de Leyburn - also a great fighting baron high in the King's favour - who in 1278 conveyed Leeds Castle, in his own words, 'to the august prince and my most dear Lord Edward the noble King of England and my fair Lady Elinor Queen of England'.

THUS BEGAN the long royal ownership of Leeds Castle and it opened brilliantly because Edward I and his Queen, Eleanor of Castile, both loved the castle and used it much as the Royal Family now use Balmoral and Sandringham. The official History of the Royal Castles states that 'the favour in which Leeds was held as a residence' by the Royal Family was shown not only by the amount of building they carried out 'but also more particularly by the occasional reference to work carried out "against the coming of the king and queen" or "in accordance with the king's own desire", by other evidence of frequent royal visits, by money laid out upon the vines, the fishponds and the park, and also by the chantry which Edward established in the castle for the soul of Queen Eleanor.' Through them also, the castle's links with the Continent were extended. Edward's mother was Eleanor of Provence and his Queen would have introduced a Spanish influence.

Edward I greatly extended the defences of the castle. The de Crèvecoeurs had relied on the natural strength of the fortifications on the islands, defended by the difficult approach to the Gate Tower and the Outer Barbican over raised causeways surrounded by water. These three embankments, guarded by gates and drawbridges, led by the Outer Barbican and the Inner Barbican to the drawbridge giving access to the Gate Tower. Once within the Gate Tower, however, there was then only an Inner Bailey, formed by walls (of which clear traces remain) leading to the main castle on the north end of the larger of the two islands. Beyond the main castle another drawbridge led to the Gloriette, the fort on the small island, where presumably the defenders would make their last stand.

This was not enough to satisfy Edward I, no doubt because he realised that if attackers came across the moat and breached the wall of the Inner Bailey, there was no further defensive position (save for a last stand in the Gloriette) and all would be lost. He enormously increased the defensive strength of the castle by adding an Outer Bailey which was enclosed by a high wall rising sheer from the water surrounding the larger island. Here five bastions or flanking towers were built, extending round the whole circuit, three on the south east and two on the north east. These bastions originally had upper storeys with spacious rooms and were almost certainly loop-holed. From them a murderous fire could be directed at besiegers trying to climb the steep walls of the Outer Bailey. Edward I also greatly enlarged and advanced the Gate Tower where the Constable of the Castle lived with his guards. The original entrance arch of the old de Crèvecoeur Gate Tower was left where it stood, however, and can still be seen today.

In those fierce times, marriage was regarded by kings and great barons almost entirely as a means of increasing or safeguarding their power and

The **Wine Cellar**, situated under the kitchens, is one of the surviving portions of the earlier Leeds Castle, built by Robert de Crèvecoeur during the early twelfth century. Wine had been produced at Leeds from even earlier times, however: the Leeds Castle vineyard was recorded in the Domesday Book in 1086. In recent years a new vineyard has been planted on the original site and Leeds Castle wine is now once again produced from the castle estates.

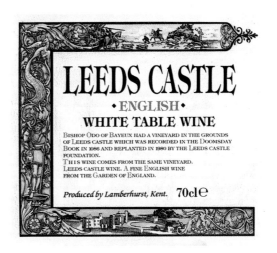

# LEEDS CASTLE
## ◆ ENGLISH ◆
### WHITE TABLE WINE

BISHOP ODO OF BAYEUX HAD A VINEYARD IN THE GROUNDS OF LEEDS CASTLE WHICH WAS RECORDED IN THE DOOMSDAY BOOK IN 1086 AND REPLANTED IN 1980 BY THE LEEDS CASTLE FOUNDATION.
THIS WINE COMES FROM THE SAME VINEYARD. LEEDS CASTLE WINE. A FINE ENGLISH WINE FROM THE GARDEN OF ENGLAND.

*Produced by Lamberhurst, Kent.*  70cl℮

The machicolated **Gate Tower** of Leeds Castle, Norman in origin but greatly extended by Edward I, bore the brunt of both the attack by King Stephen in 1139, and the siege by King Edward II almost two centuries later, after which the rebellious castellan Thomas Colepeper was hanged here. Most of the masonry dates from the end of the fourteenth century, perhaps the finest period of English castle building.

The platform, or machicolation, projecting from the top of the Gate Tower, was an important part of the castle's defences. Through the holes in the floor, boiling oil and molten lead could be poured onto the enemy besieging the gates.

wealth. It was indeed to protect the southern boundary of his French possessions in Gascony that Edward had originally married Eleanor of Castile, but gradually he grew to love her deeply and he decided to give her, as a dower, the castle where they had both spent such happy times.

Sadly, she died young, moving the King to write, 'My harp is turned to mourning, in life I loved her dearly, nor can I cease to love her in death' and, in her memory, he established a chantry in the Chapel where four canons and a clerk celebrated mass daily for her soul. The Chantry was confirmed and extended by Edward III, Richard II, Henry VI and Henry VII.

In 1299, in order to improve relations with France, Edward married Margaret, the sister of the French King Philip III, and they spent their honeymoon at Leeds Castle. The King again gave Leeds to his Queen and thus began the tradition that the castle was granted as a dower to the Queens and was retained by them during their widowhood. So from the earliest days of royal ownership Leeds became, in a sense, especially a ladies' castle.

EDWARD II, for reasons not entirely clear, granted the castle to the 'rich Lord Bartholomew de Badlesmere', an arrogant and ambitious nobleman who later joined in the conspiracies of the northern barons. When Edward's Queen Isabella, the 'she-wolf of France', sought shelter for the night at Leeds Castle in the autumn of 1321 she was deliberately seeking to test Lord Badlesmere's loyalty. His Castellan refused to admit her to the castle, ordering his archers to fire on the royal party and killing several of her guards. The King's response was to raise a feudal army of 30,000 local men and besiege the castle. After the castle was captured on 1 November, Lord Badlesmere's family were sent to the Tower. Lord Badlesmere himself was later beheaded and his head exposed on a pike on the walls of Canterbury. After her triumph Queen Isabella granted the castle to herself and held it until her death in 1358.

After the old Queen's death, Edward III carried out continuous works and enlarged the park. This work was supervised by William of Wykeham, founder of Winchester College and New College, Oxford. Extensive records of the workmen involved and their pay were kept and rates of three, four and five old pence a day were mentioned. The drawbridge was repaired and also the conduit bringing water to the Gloriette from the spring in the Park, which still supplies the castle today. The chambers of

> The **Fountain Court**, the central courtyard of the Gloriette, dates from the period of Edward III. A system was devised for bringing piped water to the fountain from springs in the park into cisterns placed beneath the paving to supply the fountain. The same springs supply the castle today.

the King and Queen Philippa of Hainault in the Gloriette were leaded and plastered. A privy wardrobe was established under its own Keeper to minister to the personal needs of the King at Leeds Castle. Further evidence reveals that in 1361 the castle boat was repaired especially for the King, and in 1365 hay was provided for the King's beds. At the latter end of the fourteenth century the royal works at Leeds Castle were supervised by Henry Yevele, the famous architect who was responsible for the nave of Canterbury Cathedral and the roof of Westminster Hall.

Richard II was another king who loved Leeds Castle and he also gave it to his Queen, Anne of Bohemia, in 1382. On her arrival at Dover in December 1381, Queen Anne had been met by John of Gaunt, Duke of Lancaster, and conducted to Leeds where she remained for the Christmas season. Even after the Queen's untimely death Richard was often there with the Court and the Privy Council, transacting important State business. Indeed on one occasion in 1394 John Elyngeham, the king's sergeant at arms, was sent to Leeds with the king's second crown. He signed the decrees against the Lollards at Leeds as well as letters patent authorising Archbishop William Courtenay to establish the Collegiate Church of All Saints in Maidstone. Here too, in 1395, he received the famous European historian Froissart, a first edition of whose *Chronicles* is at the castle. After the death of his patron, the Queen of France, Froissart came to Dover and then to Canterbury where he wrote: 'I heard that the King had gone into a beautiful Palace in Kent called Leeds Castle', and went on to describe his reception there.

At this time the issue of peace or war between England and France trembled in the balance. Both Kings wanted peace but there were strong war parties among the barons in both countries. Richard's proposal of marriage to Isabella of France was an attempt to improve relations between the two countries and they were married at Calais by the Archbishop of Canterbury in the autumn of 1396. However, Richard's reign was not without problems on the home front, too, and in 1399 he was deposed by Henry Bolingbroke, later Henry IV.

After his fall, Richard was brought back to Leeds disguised as a forester and lodged there a short time before being removed to Pontefract. Leeds therefore saw Richard both in his days of power and in his humiliation.

HENRY IV FOLLOWED the tradition by settling Leeds Castle on his Queen, Joan of Navarre, in 1403. During this time the castle underwent a general repair. Two extra rooms were made in the 'Litillond Tower' and the corbels supporting the drawbridge to 'the great tower called the Gloriett' were renewed.

In 1412 Queen Joan granted the castle, with the King's consent, to Thomas Arundel, Archbishop of Canterbury, who was the second son of

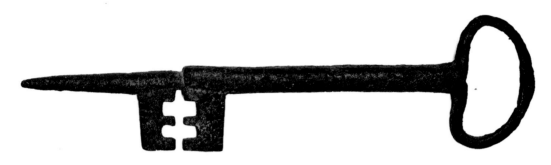

A fourteenth-century iron key recovered from the
mud near the Gate Tower when the moat was
cleaned in 1823.

Richard Fitzalan, Earl of Arundel. It was to Leeds that the Archbishop
summoned Sir John Oldcastle, Lord Cobham, the famous Lollard leader,
to stand his trial for heresy. In the words of the sentence 'he shuts himself
up in his Castle and fortifies himself…we sitting in the greater Chapel in
the Castle of Ledys, on the seat of Justice, with our Court, deemed him to
be, as in fact he was, contumacious. We then and there excommunicated
him in writing'. Lord Cobham was later beheaded. In 1414, when
Archbishop Arundel died, an inventory was taken and from it we learn for
the first time the names of the rooms in the Gloriette.

In 1416 Sigismund, the Holy Roman Emperor, the most powerful
sovereign in Europe and also the brother of Anne of Bohemia, came to
England on a State visit to Henry V, whose prestige was high after the
Battle of Agincourt. Henry made him a Knight of the Garter at Windsor
and then on 26 June the King sent his distinguished guest to Leeds Castle
where he remained for a month. Henry had meanwhile been to visit his
army at Southampton. He rejoined the Emperor at Canterbury in August
where they negotiated an offensive-defensive alliance sealed in the Treaty
of Canterbury.

After the death of his father, Henry V for a time treated Queen Joan
with great consideration and even invited her as 'Mother of the King' to
walk next to him in the celebrations of the Battle of Agincourt. But Joan
was avaricious and became very rich, and her Breton sons, from her first
marriage to the Duke of Brittany, may have intrigued against Henry V.
She had further added to her unpopularity by surrounding herself with
foreign courtiers. Suddenly she was charged with plotting the King's
death by witchcraft by the 'most high and horrible means'. We shall never
know precisely what these were because her Confessor, who had
informed against her, was strangled during a furious altercation with a
priest loyal to the Queen, enraged by the treachery against her. In the case
of Queen Joan of Navarre there was no trial, perhaps because of the death
of her accuser, but she was nevertheless imprisoned at Leeds Castle where
she had previously lived happily with Henry IV.

In the next reign, however, the King's aunt, the Duchess of Gloucester, wife of the Lord Protector of the Realm, was also accused of witchcraft and also imprisoned at Leeds Castle. The charge was that she had employed a man expert in necromancy and a woman called the 'Witch of Eye beside Winchester' to 'devise an image of wax like unto the King, the which image they dealt so with, that by their devilish incantations and sorcery, they intended to bring out of life, little and little, the King's person, as they little and little consumed that image'. This time the charge was upheld at a trial in St. Stephen's Chapel, Westminster. Later, after being remanded to Leeds Castle, she was formally condemned as a witch in the Chapel by Chichele, Archbishop of Canterbury.

In fairness to the reputation of these two royal ladies who lived at Leeds Castle 550 years ago it should be said that there is strong presumptive evidence that in both cases the charges of witchcraft were trumped up for ignoble reasons. In 1419 Henry V was acutely short of money for his French wars and coveted the rich dower of Queen Joan of Navarre. The seizure of her dower of 10,000 marks added as much as ten per cent to the general revenues of the kingdom. Just before his death the King repented and ordered her immediate release and full restoration of all her property and dignities, after which she lived peacefully and in all princely prosperity for many years. Queen Joan's detailed housekeeping accounts for living at Leeds Castle for 136 days in the year 1422 are now on display at the castle. The accounts include the expenses for the visits of the Duke of Gloucester (brother of Henry V) and Cardinal Beaufort (half-brother of Henry IV), who probably came to tell her that her persecution was ending.

The charge against the Duchess of Gloucester was really a skilful and successful attack on her husband. In the end his enemies brought the Duke down and he was charged with treason and died, perhaps murdered, in prison.

THE LAST QUEEN to own Leeds Castle personally as a dower castle was Catherine de Valois, Queen of Henry V, the victor of Agincourt. She was in fact the younger sister of Isabella, Richard II's second Queen. She received the castle in 1422 and at once repaired the Hall and other buildings. There is an inventory of this time which gives details of the prince's chamber, the great chamber in the Gloriette, the study, the cloisters and the steward's chamber.

It was during Catherine's reign that the castle's bell and clock dating from 1435 were installed. One of the oldest in the country, it strikes the hours and was rung specially when Her Majesty Queen Elizabeth II visited Leeds Castle in March 1981.

When the King died the Queen was a lively young girl of twenty-one and she soon fell in love with Owen Tudor, a handsome Welsh courtier who was Clerk of her Wardrobe and looked after her dresses and jewels. Could there be anywhere more charming and discreet for a royal romance than the gardens and park of Leeds Castle by the banks of the lake and the River Len? Discretion was indeed necessary because, when their relationship was discovered, they were both imprisoned. The Dowager Queen, however, was later released and Owen Tudor escaped from the Tower. They had, in fact, been secretly married and it was their son Edmund, Earl of Richmond, who was later to be the father of Henry VII. Thus they provided us with the Tudor dynasty whose power was finally established by Henry Tudor at the Battle of Bosworth Field. Ever since then the Crown of England has remained in the line of the heirs of the House of Tudor, which the famous historian George Macaulay Trevelyan has called 'the greatest of all the royal lines of England'.

HENRY VIII IS the most famous of all the owners of Leeds Castle. He obviously liked the castle very much, went there often and spent large sums of money in greatly enlarging and beautifying the whole range of the castle buildings. He turned Leeds from a fort into a palace but he was careful to retain all the defences of the castle, for he often had cause to fear a French invasion. He entrusted the work to the Right Hon. Sir Henry Guildford, described in 1509 as 'a lusty young man well beloved of the King'. They were boon companions who both delighted in jousts and masques, although they also shared intellectual tastes with Erasmus, the great Renaissance Humanist. The King appointed Sir Henry as Constable and Parker of Leeds in 1512. He was also a Member of Parliament, Knight

of the Garter, Master of the Horse and Comptroller of the Royal Household. He organised the English side of the Field of the Cloth of Gold, no doubt staying at Leeds Castle on the way. His portrait, painted by Holbein, is in the Royal Collection at Windsor.

The improvements made by Henry VIII were by far the most important since those made by Edward III. He transformed the Gloriette, superimposing canted bay windows of sixteen lights in the royal apartments and thoroughly repairing all the royal rooms. Repairs accounted for by the Clerk of the King's Works included tiling in the roof of the King's and Queen's apartments 'in the Glory' and the expenses of the King's glazier. In preparation for the coming of the King in 1542 the glazier supplied glass for 'the tourett over the King's lodging, the King's dining chamber, the gallery, the queen's privy chamber, the king's raying chamber, the watching chamber and the wardrobe'. Other work included decorating the King's apartments and 'pargetyng ye waylls goyng over ye drawbridge and mendying and fyllyng ye clyfts of ye walls in dyvers places about in ye howses of offys and lodgyng ther'. The King's glazier was soon at work again repairing glass 'in the stayre wyndowe going up from the king's dyning chambre up into his gracy's chambre'. This was in 1544 to prepare for a visit by Queen Catherine Parr.

The Maiden's Tower was also built around this time to house the royal Maids-of-Honour. Among these may have been Ann Boleyn who, being a Kentish girl from nearby Hever Castle, would have known well the great royal castle in Kent. A casket which belonged to Ann Boleyn is at Leeds, and the castle chapel also contains Catherine of Aragon's missal. However, apart from Ann Boleyn, it is not at present known how many of Henry VIII's other wives were at Leeds.

In 1544, after the ignominious collapse of the invasion of France by Henry VIII and Charles V, the Holy Roman Emperor, Henry retreated to England and, with the Privy Council, went straight to Leeds Castle. There the Imperial Ambassadors took their leave and, to the general consternation, were not replaced.

Besides his troubles with France and the Holy Roman Emperor, Henry VIII had serious problems in Ireland. He appointed to govern Ireland as

The **Maiden's Tower** was built in the Tudor period to house royal Maids-of-Honour, among whom, probably, was Ann Boleyn. The name, however, which dates from the nineteenth century, is a reminder that the tower was built on the site of the cell of a fourteenth-century anchorite, Christina Hyde, who lived there during the reign of Richard II.

Henry VIII, whose portrait by an unknown
English artist hangs in the castle, was its most
famous royal owner and spent large sums on its
rebuilding and enlargement.

Lord Deputy 'a wise and warie gentleman', the Right Hon. Sir Anthony
St. Leger. He pursued a conciliatory policy with the Irish, who, as a result,
agreed for the first time to accept the occupant of the English throne as
King of Ireland. Sir Anthony was Lord Deputy for twelve years, Knight of
the Garter and presided over Parliament in 1542. Henry VIII much valued
his services and decided to give him Leeds Castle as a reward although the
formal grant was not made until after Henry's death by Edward VI in 1552.

Leeds Castle thus passed out of royal ownership. For some three
hundred years it had been a principal castle of our medieval kings and
queens, many of whom loved it greatly. They and their Court were often
there as well as many princes, cardinals, ministers of state, ambassadors,
and even the Emperor of Germany, on their way between the King's
French possessions and his palace at Westminster.

Three of the Queens who owned Leeds Castle were French princesses
who brought with them the refined luxury for which the beautiful castles
of the French Royal Family were already famous. But Leeds Castle,
especially after the improvements made by Henry VIII, could rival the
beauty of these legendary French castles, many of them so marvellously
painted for the Duc de Berry and most of which, sadly, exist no more. It
was probably during the time of Henry VIII that the primitive military
function of the castle became less important and people, following the lead
of the King himself, began to feel the spell of its beauty.

The Fountain Court, prior to 1822, by William Twopenny
(*Next page*) This painting, by an unknown artist, shows the
main house built by the Smith family in 1618–30, with its
square-headed windows and leaden spouts

ONLY TWO OF Sir Anthony St. Leger's descendants lived peacefully at Leeds.
The third, Sir Warham, was not so fortunate. A financial backer of Sir
Walter Raleigh's ill-fated expedition to discover the legendary gold of El
Dorado, he was ruined when the venture ended in disaster and was forced
to sell the castle to a relative, Sir Richard Smith.

Although the Smith family were not long at the castle they did rebuild
the principal buildings at the north end of the main island. Their fine
Jacobean house, with square headed windows and leaden spouts,
survived until the middle of the eighteenth century. Passing through the
female line the castle was sold in 1632 to Sir Thomas Culpeper of
Hollingbourne who settled it on his eldest son Sir Cheney, who later took
the side of Parliament in the struggle with Charles I. During the civil war
the castle was used by Parliament as the arsenal for Kent. Because of this
and Sir Cheney's inclinations the castle was not heavily sleighted as were
the castles of Corfe and Rochester. Sir Cheney remained in possession
until his death in 1663, but the Restoration of 1660 ruined him and he died
not only deeply in debt but also intestate.

29

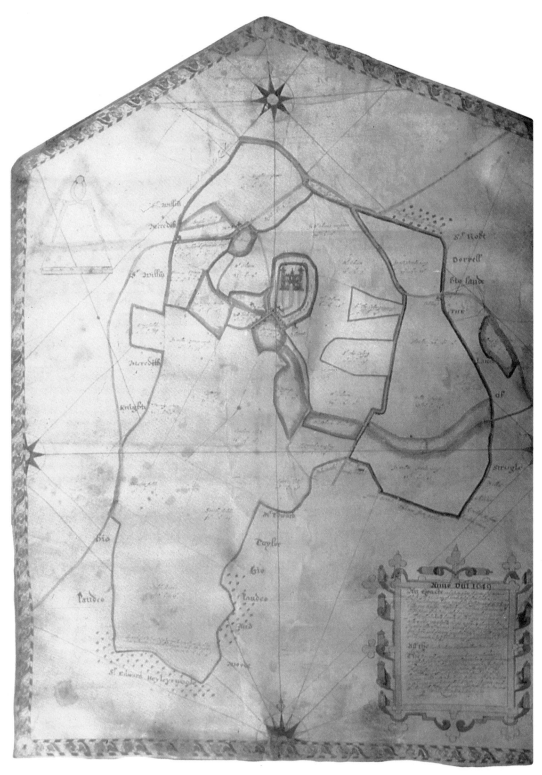

The Leeds Castle Estate Map of 1649. The Great Water can be seen below the castle building.

His cousin, Sir John Culpeper, had been an astute politician and a loyal servant of Charles I, holding the offices of both Chancellor of the Exchequer and Master of the Rolls. He had been instrumental in conveying the young Prince of Wales out of England and into exile in France and in 1649 had been rewarded for his loyalty by the gift of a large area of land in America comprising all the land between the Potomac and the Rappahanock rivers. At the time the grant was made it must have seemed worthless - indeed Lord Culpeper, who died a few weeks after the Restoration, thought so little of it that the grant is not even mentioned in his will - but it was after the Restoration that this land, totalling more than 5 million acres of Virginia, became important. It is now one of the most valuable areas in the world and contains a large part of Greater Washington.

Thomas Culpeper succeeded his father in the title and, using the dowry of his wealthy wife Margaret, purchased Leeds Castle from the creditors of Sir Cheney's estate. During his ownership, but while he was absent from the castle, Leeds was used as a prison for some 6,000 captured French and Dutch sailors. They were lodged in all parts of the castle, including the Gloriette, and on one notable occasion they actually set fire to their accommodation. This occasioned so much damage that part of the outer wall, from the angle of Henry VIII's bedroom to the conference room, collapsed into the moat and remained ruinous until 1822. A sentry box used to guard the prisoners survived until it, like so much else, was swept away in the wholesale destruction caused by the rebuilding of that year.

In charge of the prisoners for a time was the diarist John Evelyn, who wrote that, quite apart from the havoc wreaked by the inmates, the place was in need of repair and proper drains.

The sentry box used by the prison guard was recorded in a drawing made in 1822 just before it was destroyed in the rebuilding.

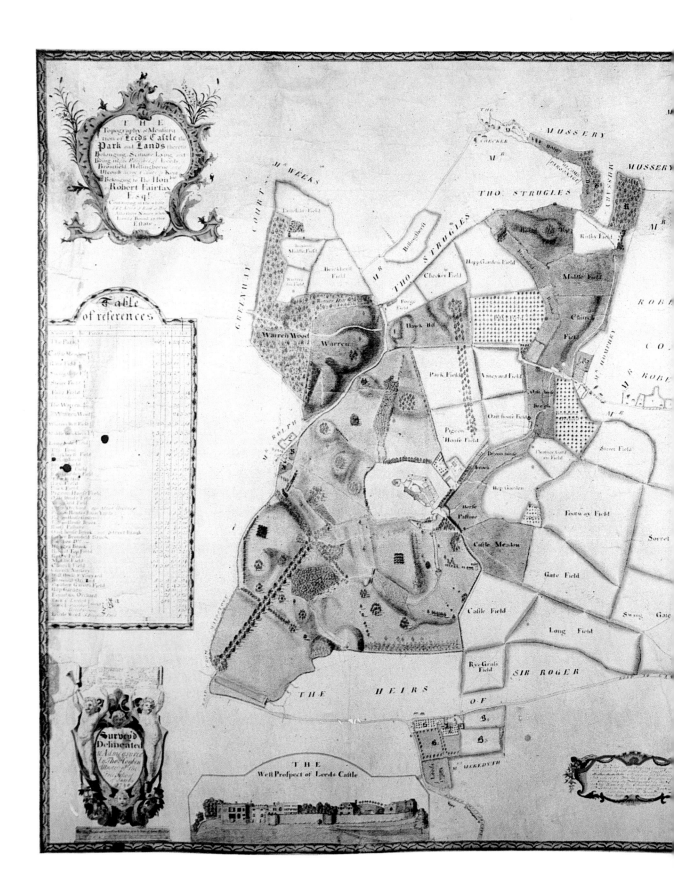

THE Topography & Mensuration of Leeds Castle the Park and Lands thereto Belonging, Scituate Lying and Being in the Parishes of Leeds, Bromfield, Hollingborne and Ulcomb in the County of Kent Belonging to the Hon.ble Robert Fairfax Esq.r

Table of references

THE West Prospect of Leeds Castle

Survey'd Delineated

34

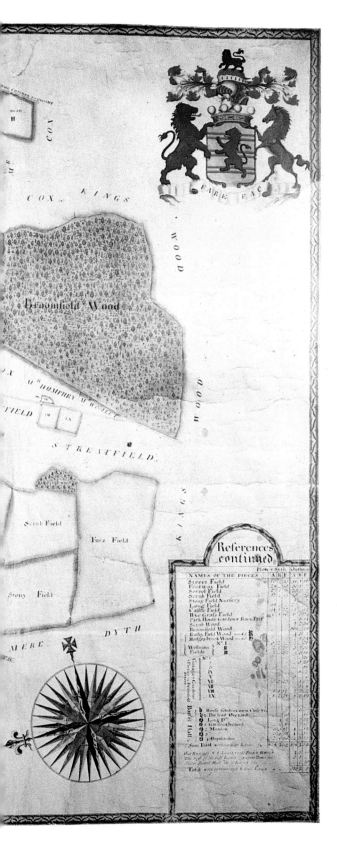

The Leeds Castle Estate Map of 1748 by Thomas Hogben, a schoolmaster who also made the sundial which stands in front of the main house. This map is one of several drawn by Hogben and is perhaps the finest example of his work. Its proper title, seen in the cartouche in the top left corner, is 'The topography and mensuration of Leeds Castle, the Park and Lands belonging to the Honble. Robert Fairfax esq. By Thomas Hogben, Master of the Free School of Smarden'. A fascinating document of local history, the map is remarkably detailed – the parish boundaries, the names of the various fields on the estate, and the names of the owners of the adjoining lands can all be clearly seen. The castle itself is drawn in block plan, while all other buildings are in perspective. The Park Gate Inn, mentioned at various times in Leeds' history and still in business today, can be seen on the left hand side close to the words 'Mr Rolph'. Hogben greatly added to the interest of his plan not only by the very elaborate cartouches and compass-rose but also by including at the bottom a panoramic view of the castle seen from the west.

In 1667 Lord Culpeper returned to Leeds but departed again some thirteen years later when, having bought out his co-proprietors in the American estate, he was appointed Governor of Virginia. His daughter, the heiress Catherine, married Thomas, 5th Lord Fairfax in the spring of 1689 and eventually, on the death of Lady Culpeper in 1709, Leeds Castle passed to the Fairfax family which had held the Propriety since 1689.

However, the American estate was by no means secure, and over the next years there was continual unrest as the settlers and the colonial government challenged the Fairfax ownership. When the 6th Lord Fairfax succeeded to his title - his extravagant father by that time having squandered most of the family fortunes and died fleeing his creditors - it had become even more crucial to secure this valuable estate, and he took steps to have his rights to sole ownership confirmed by the British Government. When this was finally sanctioned in 1745 and the government of Virginia acquiesced, Lord Fairfax sailed for Virginia, the only peer ever to emigrate to America, handing over Leeds Castle to his brother Robert.

Far from cutting him off from his old home, Fairfax's emigration served to forge the link between Leeds Castle and America which is so specially regarded today, and in his life in the new world he maintained constant reminders of his old home. He settled first with his cousin William at Belvoir on the banks of the Potomac, where he became the friend and patron of the young George Washington and indeed gave him his first job, to survey a part of the new town of Alexandria. Fairfax later decided to move nearer to the frontier in order better to supervise the development of his estates there and assigned to himself a property called 'The Manor of Leeds', of 150,000 acres - bigger by far than his original estate at Leeds Castle. At first he intended to build a new Leeds Castle in Virginia but in the end settled for a large hunting lodge called 'Greenway Court', the name of the original Culpeper house in Kent about two miles from Leeds Castle. As time went on Lord Fairfax achieved in Virginia, without seeking it, an astonishing popularity that even survived during the Revolutionary War. He took with him to America the best traditions of a good English landowner and adjusted them to suit colonial America, and it was no wonder public opinion echoed George Washington, when he mourned Lord Fairfax's death at the age of 89, and called him affectionately 'the good old Lord'.

Leeds Castle itself remained in the possession of Robert Fairfax, who was M.P. for Maidstone and Kent and who succeeded to the title as 7th Lord Fairfax. Under his ownership 'Gothick improvements' were made, in emulation of Horace Walpole's Strawberry Hill. Walpole, it seems, cast scorn on Fairfax's efforts. In 1778 he welcomed King George III and Queen Charlotte to the Castle while they were reviewing troops encamped nearby

A watercolour of the castle *c* 1790, after the 'Gothick' alterations had been made by Robert Fairfax. Comparing this painting with the one on pp. 30/1, the changes can be clearly seen, particularly in the windows.

The Fairfax family, through whom Leeds was connected for so many years with the state of Virginia, are remembered at the castle in many ways, but especially in two lasting memorials. The **Fairfax Hall**, named in their honour, is a Kentish tithe barn with a fine timbered roof, dating from 1680, the period of the first forays into the Virginia proprietary. It now makes a setting for banquets and other functions.

The **sundial** seen on the following page is an even more practical reminder of the New World, as it shows the 5-hour time difference between the Fairfax estates at Leeds and at Belvoir in Virginia. This remarkable forerunner of modern technology was designed in 1750 by a local schoolmaster, Thomas Hogben, who also drew the map of the estate dated 1748, seen on pp. 34/5.

These two pencil drawings by Eliza Wykeham-Martin show the castle before (*above*) and after (*below*) the rebuilding in 1822. In the top picture the Gothick front imposed on the building by Robert Fairfax is clearly visible.

Another drawing by Eliza Wykeham-Martin
shows the castle on 15 May 1822, the day the
foundation stone of the new building was laid.

at Maidstone. At Fairfax's death in 1793 the property passed to his nephew
Denny Martin and then, in 1800, to his brother General Philip Martin. In
1806 General Martin sold the estate in Virginia for £14,000, thus bringing
to an end the long association, and on his death a substantial part of this
fortune was left for the repair of Leeds Castle which passed, again through
the female line, to his cousin Fiennes Wykeham-Martin. By a strange
chance, he was descended from William de Leybourne, who passed the
castle to Edward I and Eleanor, and William Wykeham who strengthened
the castle's defences for Edward III. Wykeham-Martin's architect, William
Baskett of Camberwell, modernised the interior of the main building,
removed the Jacobean imprint given to the outside by Sir Richard Smith
and the 'Gothick' of Robert Fairfax, and restored the medieval style. This
was a considerable undertaking but it was achieved in a remarkably short
period of time. The foundation stones of the two entrance towers of the
main building were laid on 15 May 1822, amid great celebrations which
were reported in the local paper: 'The party afterwards partook of a cold
collation, and the workmen, to the number of nearly two hundred, were
regaled with roast beef and plum pudding and plenty of strong ale, after
which they retired very creditably, in perfect good order.' Less than four
months later, on 11 September, the roof was raised – presumably to even
greater rejoicing, as this was the 21st birthday of Wykeham-Martin's son
Charles. The following year work began on the Gloriette, and by 1824 the
castle had taken on more or less the external appearance it has today.

41

Lord Conway, the great expert in castles, in judging this restoration concluded 'it possesses one great merit..it enters perfectly into the general complex of the whole'.

With the completion of Mr. Baskett's great building works, Fiennes Wykeham-Martin had expended some £33,955 on the project and on the park improvements carried out between 1823 and 1825 - a sum approaching £3,000,000 in today's terms. The current layout of the park, with the exception of the Wood Garden, the azalea plantation and the Culpeper Garden, dates from the Wykeham-Martin era. The moat, which had been in a sorry state for many years, also took on its present appearance. New drives were cut and the principal entrance was altered to strike the road, not at the junction of the Leeds, Maidstone and Hollingbourne roads, but at the point on the Maidstone to Folkestone road where it has remained ever since.

Many of the family possessions of previous owners left Leeds around this period. In 1829 Christie's organised a large sale of furniture and pictures which are now widely dispersed. Mr. Wykeham-Martin also gave to the Strangeford family, descendants of the Smiths, all of the family portraits. These now appear to be lost. One important item, however, had a lucky escape. While the great works were in progress, an old trunk filled with Dutch tiles was purchased by a Mr. Gooding, a shoemaker of Lenham. Under the tiles he found a pile of manuscripts. Not realising their value, he began to use the documents for a variety of purposes, but fortunately Mr. John Newington Hughes, a local banker and antiquarian, heard about the manuscripts and was able to purchase them. Some time later he sold the letters to Bentley the publisher and from them was compiled the four volumes of the Fairfax correspondence.

After all the re-building and restoration at Leeds, the Wykeham-Martins settled into the round of secure ownership. The yearly migrations of the family were between properties in the Isle of Wight purchased by the 2nd Lord Culpeper in the 1660s, Chacombe Priory in Northamptonshire – the family's original home – Packwood in Warwickshire, London and Leeds. At Leeds the family were naturally the leaders of local society. Both Charles Wykeham-Martin and his son Philip were Members of Parliament; the former for Maidstone, the latter for Rochester. Philip actually died in the library of the House of Commons. Charles Wykeham-Martin's second wife was Matilda, a cousin of Anthony Trollope the novelist. He was an occasional visitor at the castle, and it is tempting to picture Leeds as the original of Courcy Castle in the Barsetshire novels.

Visitors were always welcome at the castle in groups, long before its official opening in 1976. In 1874 a small dining club of the Royal Institute of British Architects came to Leeds. Among the members of that summer excursion were F.P. Cockerell, J.H. Christian, Mr. Digby Wyatt, George Aitchison, J.L. Pearson, William Burgess and Alfred Waterhouse. Such an august group of architects must have been most interested to inspect Mr. Baskett's work at Leeds, but unfortunately there is no record of their opinions. Other guests that year were Trollope and Charles Keane, the cartoonist and illustrator of *Punch*. In August 1882 the castle witnessed the spectacle of upwards of 400 members of the Kent Archaeological Society arriving at the castle by carriage.

When the British Expeditionary Force was marching to Mons in August 1914 the officers were entertained at the castle while the Park Gate Inn on the edge of the estate did a good trade with everyone else. As the column marched off they were watched by the family from the roof of the castle.

With the death of Cornwallis Wykeham-Martin in 1924 the family was faced with such heavy death duties that the decision was made to sell and the property was put on the market. Among the prospective buyers was Randolph Hearst, the American newspaper tycoon. Already lord of his own castle in California, he was looking to acquire a similar property in England. 'WANT BUY CASTLE IN ENGLAND' read his telegram to his English agent, 'PLEASE FIND WHICH ONES AVAILABLE'. Unfortunately the report which went back to him after Leeds had been inspected was not favourable: 'QUITE UNIQUE AS ANTIQUITY BUT NEEDS EXPENDITURE LARGE SUM TO MAKE IT HABITABLE NOT A BATH IN PLACE ONLY LIGHTING OIL LAMPS SERVANTS QUARTERS DOWN DUNGEONS ...' Understandably, Hearst looked elsewhere, and in 1926 Leeds was bought by Lady Baillie, who saw through the disadvantages to the castle's true charm and character. She immediately set about its restoration with characteristic imagination and vigour, completely renovating the basic structure and restoring the Gloriette, where the most important apartments of the Kings and Queens had been in ancient times. Anglo-American by birth, Lady Baillie was brought up largely in France, and it was to that country that she turned instinctively for the designers who would transform Leeds for her. The first of these, Rateau, made a French Gothic fantasy of the Gloriette but it was Stéphane Boudin who, in the 1930s, began the task of restoring the internal harmony of the main building. Correspondence and documents of the period record the details but cannot reflect the immense enjoyment that went into the decorating and furnishing of Leeds over almost thirty years, as shopping expeditions to Paris and London, endless supplies of samples and catalogues, and long discussions finally produced the classic elegance of these rooms as we see them today. She created the Wood Garden, bordered by the little streams of the River Len, and brought rare birds from all over the world for the gardens and the lakes. Apart from the love of her children and the welfare of her staff, the embellishment of Leeds Castle became her life's work. She lived at Leeds Castle longer than any

other owner in all its recorded history, and her work for the castle ranks with that of Edward I and Eleanor of Castile, Edward III, Henry VIII and Fiennes Wykeham-Martin.

Under her care Leeds Castle became, between the wars, one of the greatest houses in England and a centre of brilliant hospitality. The young Prince of Wales, later Edward VIII and Duke of Windsor, Prince George, Duke of Kent and Princess Marina, Duchess of Kent were her guests as well as many foreign princes, ambassadors, ministers and members of parliament. But Lady Baillie was very shy and particularly disliked any personal publicity; and so Leeds Castle, in spite of its importance, was very seldom in the news.

During the second world war, Leeds figured importantly, albeit secretly, in the defence of England at her most vulnerable point, the Channel ports, which were under constant threat of invasion. The secret Petroleum Warfare Department was established to develop flame-throwing weapons, and it was from Leeds that operations were directed, largely through Mr. Geoffrey Lloyd (later Lord Geoffrey-Lloyd) reporting direct to Winston Churchill.

When the invasion crisis passed Lady Baillie gave the castle as a military hospital and herself organised a convalescent home for badly burned pilots who had been treated by the famous plastic surgeon, Sir Archibald McIndoe, at East Grinstead Hospital.

After the war, Lady Baillie lived a quiet family life and began to think more and more about the preservation of the castle for posterity. During her last illness she worked with utter determination to achieve her final purpose: to give Leeds Castle to the nation in perpetuity.

By another extraordinary historical coincidence Lady Baillie had links on both sides of her family with the castle's most famous owner Henry VIII. Her American mother came from a family whose forbears were members of the Royal Household of Henry VIII and one of whom was nominated a Knight of the Bath on the occasion of Henry VIII's marriage to Ann Boleyn. Her father was the grandson of the Marquess of Anglesey, Cavalry Commander at the Battle of Waterloo, whose ancestor was ennobled, made Secretary of State and a Knight of the Garter by Henry VIII.

Thus ancient tradition was reborn and the castle of the Queens of England was ruled for fifty years by a great lady, who then gave it to the English people for ever. In order to honour our Founder and Benefactor the Trustees of the Leeds Castle Foundation intend to maintain the long tradition that Leeds Castle is, in a special sense, a ladies' castle. To mark this, the flag of Eleanor of Castile, the first Queen to own Leeds Castle, flies from the masthead on the Tower of the Gloriette in alternation with the flag of the last personal owner of Leeds Castle, the Hon. Olive, Lady Baillie.

# The Leeds Castle Foundation

Lord Butler, a Trustee of the Foundation and at the time Master of Trinity College Cambridge, wrote on the occasion of the opening of the Castle to the public in 1976: 'Lady Baillie's imaginative and far-sighted bequest ranks with those made by the noble ladies of long ago who founded Oxford and Cambridge colleges which have now become famous centres of learning. I would stress the devotion with which the Trustees are working to fulfil Lady Baillie's vision of the role of the Foundation as a centre of Medical Research and the Arts at the highest international level with special emphasis on Anglo-American co-operation.' In fulfilling their prime charitable duty of preserving Leeds Castle in perpetuity, the Trustees will be providing for these other charitable activities a home as ancient and beautiful as the finest of the colleges at Oxford and Cambridge.

The officers of the Leeds Castle Foundation in the United Kingdom are:

*Patron*: Her Royal Highness Princess Alexandra, The Honourable Mrs Angus Ogilvy. *Chairman*: The Right Honourable Lord Aldington PC KCMG CBE DSO TD DL. The Right Honourable Lord Charteris of Amisfield GCB GCVO OBE QSO; Monsieur Gerald van der Kemp, Membre de L'Institut (France); Mrs Albert Lasker (USA); Mr Peter Mimpriss; The Honourable Angus Ogilvy; Sir David Piper CBE; The Earl of Scarbrough; Dr John Stokes MD FRCP; The Right Honourable the Lord Thomson of Monifieth KT; The Lord Walston CVO DCL; and Mr Thomas Wilcox (USA).

The Honorary Medical Advisors to the Foundation are:

Professor Sir John Butterfield OBE DM FRCP, Regius Professor of Physic at Cambridge University, and Dr John Stokes MD FRCP.

In the United States there is an associated Leeds Castle Foundation with similar objectives which has been recognised by the Internal Revenue Service as a Public Charity. The Directors of the Foundation in the United States are:

*President*: Mr Thomas R. Wilcox. Mr Lane W. Adams; Mrs William McCormick Blair, Jnr; Mrs Alice Fordyce; Mr James W. Fordyce; Mr Andrew Y. Grant; Mrs Albert Lasker; Mr William S. Paley and Mr John R. Young.

*Honorary Director*: Mrs John Hay Whitney.

A portrait of Lady Baillie with her two daughters,
painted by Drian in the 1940s, hangs in the Hall.

Many of the million and more people who have visited Leeds Castle ask,
'What was Lady Baillie really like, the woman to whom we owe all this?'

She was beautiful, intelligent, strong willed, yet shy – and above all
warmhearted. And so when she planned the preservation of her lovely
castle for the public benefit she did not want it to survive just as a dead,
stone monument; she wanted it to be the home of active, charitable work.
Her American mother's family, the Whitneys, were among the most
generous medical philanthropists in the world; she herself ran what was
really a private health service for her own staff and dependants. Her
friend, Mary Lasker, another great American medical philanthropist and
Chairman of the Albert and Mary Lasker Foundation, strongly encouraged
her interest in medical progress. She therefore decided that besides being
open to the public to enjoy its works of art, the castle should be available
to help in the fight against disease and used for medical research seminars
of the leading doctors and scientists from all nations; and that it should
become a fine conference centre. To carry out her wishes, she established
the Leeds Castle Foundation as a charitable trust.

47

To a very great extent the successful provisions of these facilities at Leeds within the first ten years of the Foundation's existence was achieved under the leadership and guidance of the late Lord Geoffrey-Lloyd, the Foundation's Chairman, and the late Mr Peter Wilson, the Foundation's first Deputy Chairman, who sadly both died in 1984. Together they strove to transform Leeds into what it is today and the Trustees would like to pay tribute to their inspired dedication.

True to the moving spirit of Lady Baillie, the Trustees encourage the castle's use for medical research seminars and want visitors to be received in a way that she herself would have approved. To do this they have continued to improve the amenities in the castle and the park while preserving Leeds' great beauty. They have provided special facilities for the disabled, developed the Culpeper Garden, established a vineyard on the site of one recorded in the Domesday Book and recreated the Great Water which in the Middle Ages was an important part of the castle's defences. The Trustees have also made the castle one of the world's finest conference centres.

The castle was opened to the public on 1 July 1976 by Her Royal Highness Princess Alexandra, Patron of the Foundation. Seen with Her Royal Highness are (*left to right*) Mrs Remington-Hobbs (daughter of Lady Baillie), Lord Geoffrey-Lloyd and Mr Peter Wilson.

48

True to its historical tradition as the castle of queens, Leeds has received many royal visitors in recent years. Her Majesty the Queen visited Leeds in 1981 and was shown round the castle and the park.

In the summer of 1984 the castle welcomed Her Royal Highness Princess Anne, President of the Save the Children Fund, at a special children's day.

Leeds has also provided a secure and private venue for meetings and conferences of international stature. In July 1978 the Foreign Ministers of America, Egypt and Israel met at Leeds for the vital Middle East peace talks: (*left to right*) Mr Cyrus Vance, Mr Mohammed Ibrahim Kamel and General Moshe Dayan.

Throughout the year Leeds Castle plays host to many different special events, the most spectacular of which is the open-air concert (*left*) with a closing firework display (*below*).

(*Opposite page*) The castle by moonlight.

*Above* Children from a local primary school perform the traditional maypole dance at the Leeds craft fair. *Right* Beating the Retreat in front of the castle.

# The Park

Much of the castle's charm is due to its island setting, although it was originally very much the defensive possibilities of a castle surrounded naturally by water which inspired its construction. The moat was of supreme importance, but another vital part of the castle's defences was the second lake, the **Great Water**. This lake, of some six acres, which can be seen on the estate map of 1649 (page 32), could be drained in more peaceful times to become a water meadow, and over the centuries has seemed to appear and disappear at different times. In 1979 the Great Water was restored to its former splendour by Russell Page and now forms a natural feature of the landscape as it did in medieval times. The lake can still be drained and refilled quite quickly, just as the Plantagenet engineers intended, by the use of a medieval sluice in the dyke near the Gate Tower.

The **Wood Garden** and the **Duckery** are two of the less formal areas of the park where the landscape, although carefully planned, has been allowed to develop more freely, partly in order to provide a habitat for the waterfowl which roam freely over the whole area. The initial landscaping of the Wood Garden was done in the 1920s, to make the most of the natural beauty of the streams of the River Len flowing through the park. It was conceived from the start as a 'green garden' and more particularly as a 'Spring garden', with large areas of daffodils, narcissi and anemones planted among the native ash, willows and alder, making the area especially colourful in springtime. The **Duckery** was created by Stéphane Boudin and Russell Page in the 1960s from a wilderness of tangled brambles and fallen trees, and now forms a perfect habitat for the fowl but also an idyllic spot for their owner. From the shaded seat in the Pavilion, one of the most beautiful views of the castle can be seen. The first inhabitants of the Duckery were eleven birds bought by a sympathetic Lady Baillie from a lady who had to give up her collection. Always a bird-lover, Lady Baillie also had the passion and initiative of a true collector, and in a short time had amassed a fine collection of waterfowl, ranging from mallard and teal to Canada geese and the elegant black swans.

The **Culpeper Garden** was created in
1980 by Russell Page on an oddly-
shaped sloping plot of land which
for hundreds of years had served as
a vegetable plot or kitchen garden. It
is named after the Culpeper family,
owners of Leeds in the seventeenth
century and first owners of the
Virginia estate. This enclosed garden
is framed on three sides by the warm
red brick of old estate buildings and
a high wall, while the remaining side
looks out over the Great Water. The
flower beds, edged with low box
hedges, are arranged in formal
pattern and separated by brick
pathways, so that visitors have the
impression of walking through a
field of flowers. The flowers
themselves are those of an old
English cottage garden - roses,
pinks, lad's love and lavender,
poppies and lupins - but with some
more exotic blooms mingled among
the old favourites, and all with
wonderful scents, which makes this
garden such a delight for the blind.
As a final touch, a herb garden has
been planted along the old wall;
something which might have
pleased a later namesake, the
famous seventeenth-century
herbalist Nicholas Culpeper.

A Princess of Wales Parrakeet with two youngsters - typical of the Australian parrakeets which were the great interest of Lady Baillie.

The first aviaries at Leeds Castle were established over twenty-five years ago to house Lady Baillie's collection of small Australian finches. Over the years her enthusiasm brought many rare and varied species to the castle, and she developed a special interest in parrakeets, particularly the Australian and Ringneck varieties. At the time of her death in 1974 the collection contained most of the Australian species and many colour mutation Ringnecks, most of these being bred successfully in the aviaries. Other birds have been introduced in recent years, including macaws, cockatoos and love-birds, but the parrakeets have remained the centrepiece of the collection. Because of their shyness, some of the parrakeets are not on show but continue to breed in private, making Leeds one of the major centres in the country for the study of these species.

A female Eclectus (*right*), native of
Australia, New Guinea and Indonesia.
The male of this species is all green - a
striking contrast.

Peacocks (*above*), can be seen roaming
all over the park.

Leadbeater's or Major Mitchell's
Cockatoo (*right*) from Australia is one
of the most beautiful members of the
cockatoo family.

The colourful blooms being cultivated in the greenhouses at
Leeds are matched by the wide range of plants found in the
outdoor beds. The warm, sunny shelter of the old brick
wall is ideal for both the herb plants growing in the border
and for the espalier pear tree.

Dogs have always been present at Leeds Castle throughout the ages – hounds for hunting, gundogs, mastiffs to guard the castle gates, spaniels and lapdogs to grace the apartments of the widowed queens. Lady Baillie was never without several dogs, and it is only fitting that Leeds should now house what is beyond doubt the finest collection of antique dog collars in the world. The collection, which ranges over four hundred years, was most generously presented to the Leeds Castle Foundation by Mrs Gertrude Hunt in memory of her husband John hunt, the distinguished medievalist.

*Above and below right*: collars in leather, bronze, brass and silver to suit all kinds of dog, are displayed in the collection. *Below left*: a German portrait of two dogs, *c* 1800.

Description of the Rooms

In the nineteenth century the chamber which is now the **Heraldry Room** used to be the Great Hall of the castle, and in this century Lady Baillie added to its natural grandeur by installing an impressive Jacobean-style ceiling. The room now encapsulates the whole history of Leeds. It contains the coats of arms of many of the owners of the castle from King Ethelbert IV to Lady Baillie, along with portraits and miniatures, and historical memorabilia relating to the families associated with Leeds from the sixteenth to the nineteenth centuries. This collection, which includes many items owned by members of the Culpeper, Fairfax, and Wykeham families, was generously bequeathed to the Foundation by the late Mr Fiennes Fairfax Wykeham-Martin.

The portraits are of (*above left*) Catherine Fairfax, the 'Culpeper heiress' whose marriage to Lord Fairfax ultimately brought Leeds Castle to the Fairfax family and (*above right*) Robert Fairfax, into whose care the castle was entrusted when the 6th Lord emigrated to Virginia. The other items are (*right*) the Culpeper ivory seal, with the family arms, and (*below*) a jewel box thought to have been owned by Ann Boleyn and left behind by her after a visit to the castle.

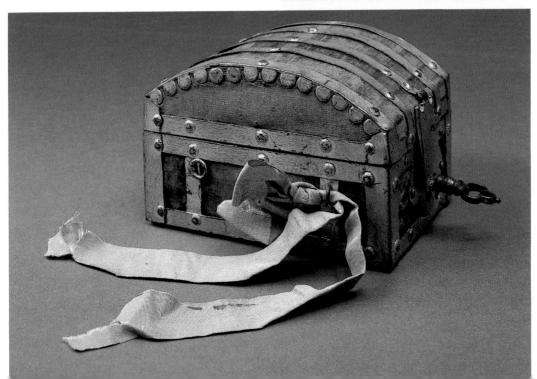

**Les Chambres de la Reine** take us back to the fifteenth century, showing the two rooms as they might have been prepared for Catherine de Valois and re-creating the splendour and luxurious surroundings such a royal lady would have enjoyed. Every detail of the reconstruction is authentic and is based on documents and manuscript illustrations of the period, such as the one below. All the furniture in these rooms has been made in the same materials and by the same methods as would have been used in the fifteenth century.

The larger of the two rooms is known, as in the fifteenth century, as la Chambre de ma Dame. The splendour of these rooms was a means of expressing the rank and title of their occupant, and the symbolism of the various items of furniture was vital. The **state bed**, of enormous size, was never meant to be slept in but was simply a means of indicating the Queen's status; the Queen would have slept in another room. Likewise, the height of the silk-draped **state chair** was to enable her to keep her head above the level of those standing in attendance.

The other piece of furniture in the Chambre de ma Dame serves a more practical purpose. The **day-bed** standing before the fireplace has wheels so that it could be moved nearer to the warm fire if needed. This second bed also has a high, cone-shaped canopy, called a sparver, which is surmounted by a golden crown – another popular means of ensuring that all eyes were drawn towards the Queen. The hand-made tapestry carpet beneath the bed is copied from the one in the illustration (previous page).

The silk damasks with which the walls and furniture are hung were woven specially with a design symbolizing the marriage of Catherine and Henry V, the initials H and C tied with a lover's knot. This design, worked on the wall hangings in green and gold, is repeated, in red and gold and rather smaller, in the other furnishings. The use of the initials helps to emphasise the very personal nature of this part of the castle. These magnificent fabrics, another vital symbol of power and precedence, conceal not only the stone walls of the chamber but also the very basic nature of the furniture. For beneath the splendid silks, the fine linen sheets and the feather and straw mattresses, the bed and the chair are of the plainest unpolished wood and the simplest construction. This was necessary because, when the Queen was not in residence, the bed would be dismantled and the fine hangings folded away.

Small and comfortable, with a fireplace, the **chambre de retrait** shows the kind of arangements made for bathing in any place where a stone bath was not a permanent fixture. Etiquette and courtly splendour were just as important in the bathroom as anywhere else, and here again the walls are hung with damask. The design matches that of the fabric in the main room but here it is worked in green and red. Like the state bed in the Chambre de ma Dame, the bath itself is surprisingly humble beneath its hangings – a simple wooden cooper's tub, standing on a rush mat. The tub is hung about with a fine white circular curtain which hangs from a sparver canopy, again denoting rank, suspended from the ceiling. Like the state bed, this was all designed to be easily dismantled when the Queen was not in residence. The towels hanging over the sides of the bath are of the finest white linen and were intended to protect the royal user from the rough wood surface. Inside the bath is a wooden stool, also draped in linen, for the Queen to sit on, and another stands outside to assist her in stepping in and out. The bath would have been filled with herb-scented water, carried up from the kitchens in wooden buckets, and emptied through the tap which can be seen at the base.

Triptych by the Master of the St. Ursula Legend

The **Queen's Gallery** leading into the Fountain Court not only has a fine carved oak ceiling but houses several examples of oak furniture from different periods, such as the sixteenth-century Florentine wardrobe seen below. The fireplace, carved in Kent ragstone, was at one time fitted in another room in the castle but was reinstated here by Lady Baillie. A pair of Brussels tapestries on biblical themes hang on the walls but perhaps the most important work in the chamber is the sixteenth-century triptych by the Master of the St. Ursula legend, showing the Virgin and Child surrounded by saints and, in the left panel, the donor.

The **Henry VIII Banqueting Hall**, with its superb ebony wood floor and carved oak ceiling, runs a length of seventy-five feet between the Chapel and the Gallery along the western side of the castle. The bow window is one of several features dating from Sir Henry Guilford's supervision of rebuilding for Henry VIII in 1517. The fireplace is of particular interest: the sixteenth-century chimneypiece is French, of carved stone with medallion busts in relief, and was brought to the castle by Lady Baillie during the extensive rebuilding of 1926-8, while the actual fireback is one of the earliest known in England, dating perhaps from the period of Edward IV. The refectory table, from the early seventeenth century, came from a monastery near Chartres, and has drawers in which the monks would have kept their cutlery. Above this hangs a wall carpet made to Persian design in India around 1600, while the Flemish tapestry seen on the far wall was probably woven shortly before 1500 and portrays the *Adoration of the Magi*. Tapestries woven before 1500 are rare, and this one is a particularly fine example. The painting of the *Adoration of the Shepherds* hanging above the oak chest is by Del Maino, and of the other paintings in the room, perhaps the most impressive is the Cranach *Adam and Eve*.

75

This early sixteenth-century Brussels tapestry, woven in silks and particularly rich metallic threads, shows St Jerome accompanied by his lion. The *Adam and Eve* by Lucas Cranach, also from the sixteenth century, is one of the masterpieces of the German Renaissance. Cranach was one of the first northern European painters to treat the nude as a suitable subject for painting in the humanist tradition.

The chapel organ is thought to have been built by
Robert and William Gray in 1796 for Spencer
Perceval, the Prime Minister assassinated in 1812.

The **Chapel**, reconsecrated for worship in 1978 by the Archbishop of Canterbury, is a simple building with windows decorated with Kentish tracery, dating from the thirteenth century. The walls are hung with Venetian canvas printed locally with a Gothic design while the altar-frontal is a fifteenth-century tapestry from a church near Strasbourg. Four large hanging panels, showing the Annunciation, the Nativity, the Adoration of the Magi and the Circumcision, are thought to be the work of Ulm woodcarvers of the early sixteenth century. The silver cross on the altar was donated by the Royal College of Nursing, and a niche in the south wall contains a treasury of other items.

The sixteenth-century **Gothic oak staircase** was
brought from France by Lady Baillie in order to
give access to the first floor at this end of the
castle. It is built entirely of oak, with solid oak
steps and a central fluted newel post carved from
a single tree trunk. The handrail, carved from the
trunk, ends in the figure of a crusader. On the
landing at the head of the stairs hangs a group of
pen and wash sketches by Constantin Guys,
whose vignettes of fashionable society in
nineteenth-century Paris reflect the flamboyance
and extravagance of the Second Empire. The
sketches were bequeathed to the Foundation by
Lord Geoffrey-Lloyd.

Eugène Boudin: **Beach Scene**

It is in the **seminar room** that the many medical and scientific conferences to which Leeds Castle has been host have taken place. Here, too, in 1978, the Foreign Ministers of Egypt, Israel and America met for the vital preliminary talks which led to the signing of the Peace Treaty at Camp David later that year. Housed in this room is one of the finest collections of Impressionist paintings in the country, with works by Degas, Pissarro and Vuillard. The delightful beach scene by Boudin - a work in his most esteemed style - is from Lady Baillie's own collection, as is the Toulouse-Lautrec sketch of the dancer Gabrielle. Presiding over the room from its place in the window is an Egyptian bronze cat from the Saite period, about 600 B.C. Originally, this probably served as a mummy-case for this sacred animal.

A view along the corridor which links the
Gloriette to the later part of the castle.

Italian stone lion

Detail from a Flemish hunting tapestry

The **hall**, with its stone-flagged floor and Gothic
arches, is dominated by a large stone lion, holding
a lamb between its front paws, which dates from
the late twelfth century. A familiar feature of the
Romanesque churches of northern Italy
(outstanding examples are at Parma Cathedral
and San Zeno in Verona), it originally formed the
base of one of the columns of a portico. The walls
of the upper storey of the hall are hung with
tapestries, including this fine Flemish hunting
tapestry from the sixteenth century, in which
hounds and beasts crouch and bound among the
woodland thickets.

The **Yellow Drawing Room** brings together a Russian carpet, English furniture, Chinese and Japanese porcelain and French and Italian painting, in what is one of the most harmonious colour schemes in the castle. The carpet was made by monks at a St. Petersburg monastery in the early nineteenth century. The furniture includes a Queen Anne lacquer table, William and Mary chairs with embroidered upholstery, and a pair of early nineteenth-century ebony and ormulu bookcases, one either side of an eighteenth-century marble chimneypiece. Carrying through the motif of birdlife already seen in other rooms, a pair of Japanese porcelain hawks on the chimneypiece and Chinese cranes set on brackets on the wall are a reminder of Lady Baillie's favourite form of collecting. On either side of the fireplace hang flower paintings by the French artist Monnoyer with, between them, *Pulchinelli enjoying an alfresco meal* by Tiepolo. This painting is one of several by the artist featuring the Commedia del'Arte figure in realistic contemporary settings.

G.B. Tiepolo: *Pulchinelli enjoying an alfresco meal*

Bowl, jug and dish from the mother-of-pearl collection formed by Lady Baillie

**The Thorpe Hall room** is an outstanding example of English mid-seventeenth-century decorative art. The marble fireplace and the wood panelling were taken from Thorpe Hall near Peterborough, designed in 1653 by Peter Mills for Chief Justice St. John, and were installed in Leeds Castle in 1927 by Lady Baillie. Peter Mills was one of the architects, along with Sir Christopher Wren, commissioned to supervise the rebuilding of London after the great fire of 1666. The doorway of the Thorpe Hall room, with its composition of volutes, pilasters, garlands and panels, typifies seventeenth-century woodcarving at its best.

The carpet is English, an armorial design from 1745, and the furniture is also mostly of the eighteenth century, with fine examples of both English and French workmanship. A clock, with Vincennes figure with elaborate Louis XV ormulu mounts, is one of only two surviving examples of their kind in the world. The bird-life which features everywhere at Leeds is also found here, in the collection of Chinese porcelain: phoenix, pheasants and a pair of brown ducks.

Stéphane Boudin designed for Lady Baillie a suite of rooms, many of which are now used by the Foundation for the accommodation of conference members and as such are unfortunately not available for public viewing. Although some redecoration has been necessary and some items of furniture have been replaced, the spirit of the rooms has been kept intact.

The **Library**, still furnished very much as it was in Lady Baillie's day, was based on a design in a seventeenth-century engraving. With its walls lined with glowing leather-bound volumes and its fine Georgian fireplace, it still retains the comfortable and relaxed air of a private reading room. In fact, it is now often used as an assembly room for guests about to move into the adjoining Dining Room. Like many of the other private rooms, the **Dining Room** reflects the Anglo-French taste of both its designer and its former owner.

All the bedrooms at Leeds were designed to be quite
different in character and each has its own furnishing
scheme and colour scheme, as reflected in the names –
the Blue Room, the Green Room and so on. This gave
Boudin and Lady Baillie a chance to indulge different
aspects of their interests. In the Green Room, for
example, a particular feature was made of old fabrics –
panels of appliqué work acquired from various sources
were refashioned into bed-hangings and wall panels. In
the **Cream Room** the very restrained use of colour shows
off particularly the prints on the walls and the furniture.
Of especial interest is a highly unusual painted commode
on the right of the fireplace, executed especially for Lady
Baillie.

As is fitting, the grandest of all the bedrooms, the **Blue Room**, is the one which was used by Lady Baillie herself. The white bed, with its high canopy and hangings embroidered with an eighteenth-century design, dominates the room, but the other striking feature is the panelling. This is a superb example of Boudin's skill with wood-finishing and was produced by a special process which entailed bringing up the grain by rubbing with a wire brush, then applying layers of thin glaze and finally rubbing in dry colour and waxing. There are still many echoes of Lady Baillie in the room, especially in the choice of the Chinese porcelain birds mounted on brackets on the walls.

*Acknowledgments*

The publishers would like to thank the following people for their contributions to the text:

David Cleggett                                                    The late Lord Geoffrey-Lloyd
Jonathan Keates                                                  The late Peter Wilson, CBE

The map on p.5 was drawn by Dennis Hawkins.

Most of the photographs were taken by Angelo Hornak, with the exception of the following:

John Vere Brown, pp.66, 68, 70/1                         Sloman and Pettitt, p.48
Peter Coates, p.61 (*below right*)                          Alex Starkey, p.95
Barrie Duffield Photography, pp.49 (*right*), 50      Andy Williams, p.55(*top right*),
Paul Hillman, pp.40, 41                                              56/7, 59(*peacock*), 61

For permission to reproduce illustrations the publishers are grateful to the following:

The Dowager Lady Anson, pp.33, 40, 41                 Interiors Magazine, pp.66, 68, 70/1
The British Library, p.67                                          Kent County Archives, pp.32, 34/5
The British Museum, p.29                                        The Press Association, p.49(*lower left*)
Country Life Magazine, p.95

The painting on pp.30/1 is in a private collection and we are most grateful to the owners for allowing us to photograph it.